Conspiracy Thinking

Why Facts Alone Rarely Change Minds

Conspiracy Thinking

Why Facts Alone Rarely Change Minds

Conspiracy Thinking:
Why Facts Alone Rarely Change Minds

Richard Rawson, Psy.D., MBA

© 2026 Richard Rawson
All rights reserved.

No part of this book may be reproduced, stored, or transmitted in any form or by any means without the prior written permission of the author, except for brief quotations used in reviews or scholarly works.

This book is intended for educational and informational purposes only. It does not constitute professional, legal, or clinical advice.

ISBN: 979-8-9946881-2-0

Published by Rawson Internet Marketing.
United States of America.

Table of Contents

Chapter 1: The Wrong Question 1

Chapter 2: What Conspiracy Thinking Does 7

Chapter 3: Normal Minds in Abnormal Conditions 13

Chapter 4: The Emotional Economy of Belief 21

Chapter 5: Identity, Role, and Belonging 27

Chapter 6: How These Beliefs Are Maintained 33

Chapter 7: Two Ethical Domains 39

Chapter 8: Truth, Harm, and the Limits of Correction . . . 45

Chapter 9: When Harm Requires Intervention 49

Chapter 10: When to Challenge and When Not To 55

Chapter 11: Indirect Interventions 61

Chapter 12: Preserving Relationships 67

Chapter 13: What Real Change Looks Like 71

Chapter 14: Why Debunking Culture Backfires 75

Chapter 15: Building Psychological Resilience 83

Chapter 16: What This Book Ultimately Argues 87

The Wrong Question

CHAPTER 1
The Wrong Question

THE WRONG QUESTION

The Wrong Question

Most conversations about conspiracy thinking begin with a familiar question: Why do people believe false things? It sounds reasonable. It sounds scientific. It sounds like the kind of question that should lead to better explanations and better solutions. It carries the assumption that if we can identify the cause of error, we can fix it. But that assumption points us in the wrong direction, because it frames the problem as one of information and misunderstanding rather than one of function and meaning.

The question presumes that the central problem is ignorance or misunderstanding. It treats conspiracy belief as a failure of information, a breakdown in reasoning, or a lack of exposure to the right evidence. From there, the solution seems straightforward. Provide better facts. Correct the mistakes. Explain more clearly. The underlying expectation is that if people just understood, they would change. In practice, that is not what happens, and the persistence of these beliefs even after repeated correction tells us something important about what is really going on.

In many cases, people who hold conspiracy beliefs have already encountered the relevant information. They have seen the counterarguments. They have heard the corrections. Often, they can summarize those corrections accurately. They are not unaware of what mainstream explanations say. And yet the belief remains. In some cases, it becomes more entrenched after being challenged. This is not a small communication failure; it is a signal that the frame itself is wrong and that something other than simple error correction is at work.

If false belief were mainly a problem of missing information, then education would reliably fix it. If it were mainly a problem of faulty reasoning, then clearer logic would consistently help. Instead, what we see, again and again, is that more information often produces more resistance. Correction can harden positions. Evidence becomes something to argue against rather than something to integrate, which is not how ordinary error behaves in most areas of life.

When people make a simple mistake in arithmetic, they usually accept the correction. When they misunderstand a factual detail, clarification tends to resolve it. Conspiracy thinking does not follow that pattern. It responds differently because it is doing something different, and that difference is the key to understanding why facts alone so often fail to change minds.

Conspiracy beliefs are often treated as claims that can be evaluated in isolation. A person says something about a hidden plot, a corrupt institution, or a coordinated deception, and the response is to examine the evidence for that specific claim. That approach makes sense if the belief is primarily about the claim itself. But in many cases, the claim is only the surface. Underneath it is a broader way of organizing experience, one that gives shape to fear, anger, confusion, and loss of trust.

From the outside, a conspiracy belief looks like a statement about the world. From the inside, it often functions more like a story that explains why things feel the way they do. It offers a cause for distress. It identifies agents who can be blamed. It turns diffuse unease into a narrative with villains, motives, and intentions. In doing so, it reduces randomness and replaces uncertainty with explanation, even if that explanation is deeply flawed.

This is why belief and identity so often become intertwined. For some people, holding the belief is not just about agreeing with a claim. It is about being the kind of person who sees what others miss. It is about being vigilant rather than naïve, skeptical rather than fooled, awake rather than asleep. Those are not trivial self-descriptions. They carry moral and emotional weight. They become part of how someone understands who they are in a world they no longer trust.

When belief is serving that role, it cannot be treated as a detachable error. Challenging it is not just a matter of correcting a detail. It is experienced as a challenge to judgment, character, and identity. The correction does not land as neutral information. It lands as a threat to the person's standing, competence, or moral position. That is why people so often respond defensively, even when the evidence is strong and even when they can follow the logic.

This also helps explain why conversations about conspiracy thinking so quickly become emotionally charged. The discussion is rarely just about data. It is about who is credible, who is naïve, who is corrupt, and who is being deceived. Once those stakes are in play, disagreement stops being a technical matter and starts being a relational and moral one. At that point, doubling down on facts often intensifies the conflict rather than resolving it.

Debunking culture is built on the assumption that exposure to the right information is the primary intervention. Articles, videos, and social media threads are designed to expose falsehoods, list errors, and demonstrate contradictions. In some cases, that approach works, particularly when beliefs are loosely held and not tightly bound to identity or emotion. But when belief is functioning as a stabilizing structure, debunking does something different. It raises the cost of letting go.

If abandoning the belief would mean losing a sense of competence, losing a moral position, or losing a community of like-minded people, then the belief becomes something to protect. Evidence is no longer just information. It becomes something to interpret, resist, or reframe in order to preserve the structure. At that point, even strong counterevidence can be absorbed in a way that strengthens the belief rather than weakens it.

This is why people sometimes become more committed after being challenged. The challenge forces a choice between the belief and the person's sense of self. When those are aligned, defending the belief feels like defending one's integrity. That is not a failure of intelligence. It is a predictable response when beliefs are carrying identity and emotional load.

None of this means that facts are irrelevant or that truth does not matter. It means that truth is not operating in a vacuum. It is interacting with fear, shame, loyalty, and self-concept. When those forces are strong, accuracy alone is often too weak a lever to move the system. In some cases, it even makes the system more rigid by increasing the perceived threat.

The common response to this observation is to assume that people who hold conspiracy beliefs must be unusually irrational, emotionally fragile, or intellectually deficient. That assumption is comforting because it locates the problem in a small, defective group. It allows everyone else to imagine that better reasoning would solve the issue if only those people were more open-minded.

The reality is more uncomfortable. Many people who hold conspiracy beliefs are otherwise competent, functional, and capable in most areas of life. They work, raise families, manage businesses, and make complex decisions. The belief exists alongside those capacities, not in place of them. That fact alone should make us suspicious of explanations that rely solely on stupidity, pathology, or simple cognitive failure.

What makes more sense is to treat conspiracy thinking as a response to conditions that feel intolerable, confusing, or threatening. It is a way of imposing structure on chaos. It is a way of restoring a sense of control when institutions feel untrustworthy and outcomes feel arbitrary. It is a way of locating meaning when events seem random or unfair.

When seen in that light, the question shifts. The central issue is no longer just why people believe false things. The more important issue is what those beliefs are helping them manage and what would happen if those beliefs were suddenly removed. Without understanding that, attempts to correct are likely to miss the real problem and, in some cases, make it worse.

This is why facts alone so often fail to change minds in this domain. They are addressing the surface while leaving the underlying structure intact. In some cases, they destabilize that structure without offering a replacement. When that happens, people do not simply update their beliefs. They defend the structure that has been helping them cope.

This book is not an argument against truth or evidence. It is an argument for understanding what belief is doing before trying to take it away. It is an argument for recognizing that in many cases, conspiracy thinking is not just a mistake to be corrected. It is a psychological solution to a different problem, one that facts alone are not designed to solve.

That recognition does not make the beliefs true. It does not excuse harm. It does not mean that anything goes. It means that if the goal is to reduce damage, preserve relationships, and create conditions where change is actually possible, then starting with function rather than error is not a concession. It is a necessity.

CHAPTER 2
What Conspiracy Thinking Does

What Conspiracy Thinking Does

What Conspiracy Thinking Does

Conspiracy thinking is often discussed as if it were mainly a set of incorrect beliefs about the world. In that framing, the task is to identify which claims are false and replace them with more accurate ones. That approach treats belief as a kind of data storage problem. The person has the wrong file, and the solution is to upload the correct one.

But for many people, conspiracy thinking is not primarily about storing information. It is about regulating experience. It is a way of making uncertainty tolerable, of giving shape to threat, and of restoring a sense of coherence when the world feels unpredictable or hostile. To understand why these beliefs persist, it helps to look at the functions they serve rather than only at the claims they contain.

One of the most powerful functions is the reduction of uncertainty. Modern life is saturated with complexity. Systems are opaque. Institutions are distant. Decisions are made by people most citizens will never meet, using processes that are difficult to see or understand. For many people, this produces a chronic sense that important things are happening beyond their reach and beyond their comprehension. Conspiracy narratives offer a way to collapse that complexity into a simpler story. Instead of faceless systems and diffuse forces, there are identifiable actors with motives and intentions. The world becomes smaller and more legible, even if it becomes more sinister in the process.

That tradeoff is often emotionally preferable to randomness. A malicious agent can be hated, blamed, and resisted. Pure contingency cannot. When bad outcomes are attributed to chance, incompetence, or structural forces, people are left with few clear targets and little sense of agency. A conspiracy narrative, however flawed, restores a sense that someone is in control and that there is a logic behind what is happening. That can be perversely reassuring, even when the logic is dark.

Another function is the restoration of agency. Many conspiracy beliefs frame the believer as someone who sees through deception. The person is no longer a passive recipient of official narratives. They become an active interpreter, someone who uncovers hidden truths and resists manipulation. This position can feel empowering, particularly for people who otherwise feel ignored, marginalized, or powerless in institutional contexts. The belief does not just explain the world. It elevates the believer's role within it.

This sense of agency is closely tied to identity. For some, being skeptical of official accounts becomes a defining feature of who they are. It is not just something they believe. It is how they understand themselves in relation to authority, expertise, and social norms. They are not sheep. They are not fooled. They are not naïve. These self-descriptions carry emotional and moral weight. They offer a way to maintain self-respect in environments where trust feels risky and vulnerability feels dangerous.

Conspiracy thinking also serves a social function. Beliefs are rarely held in isolation. They are shared, reinforced, and elaborated within communities, whether online, in families, or in social networks organized around common grievances or identities. These communities provide validation. They provide a sense of belonging. They provide a shared language for interpreting events. In some cases, the social bond is as important as the belief itself.

When someone is part of such a community, abandoning the belief is not just a private cognitive shift. It can mean losing relationships, losing status, and losing a sense of shared reality. The belief is embedded in a social world. Challenging it can feel like betraying that world. This makes change more costly and defense more likely, even in the face of strong counterevidence.

Conspiracy narratives also provide moral structure. They divide the world into good and evil, victims and perpetrators, insiders and outsiders. This can be especially appealing in times of moral confusion or institutional failure, when traditional sources of authority and legitimacy are widely distrusted. The conspiracy story offers a clear map. It identifies who is responsible for harm and who is innocent. It transforms complex social problems into conflicts between intentional actors.

This moral clarity can be psychologically stabilizing. It reduces ambiguity. It simplifies responsibility. It allows people to locate themselves on the side of the righteous, even when they feel powerless to change the larger system. In that sense, the belief does not just explain events. It justifies emotional reactions. Anger, suspicion, and withdrawal become not only understandable but morally appropriate.

Another important function is emotional containment. Many conspiracy beliefs organize fear, grief, and rage into a coherent narrative. When people experience loss, betrayal, or sustained disappointment with institutions, those emotions can feel overwhelming and diffuse. A conspiracy story gathers them into a single explanation. The emotion now has a cause. The cause has a face. The feeling becomes anchored to a narrative that can be repeated and shared.

This containment does not make the emotions disappear, but it makes them more manageable. They are no longer just free-floating distress. They are responses to a story. In that sense, the belief acts like a psychological container. Removing it without addressing the underlying emotion can leave the person more destabilized, not less.

All of these functions mean that conspiracy thinking is often doing real psychological work. It is providing coherence, agency, identity, community, moral structure, and emotional containment. That does not make the beliefs accurate. It does not make them harmless. But it does explain why they are resistant to simple correction.

When a belief is performing multiple stabilizing functions, taking it away is not like correcting a typo. It is more like removing a load-bearing wall. Without an alternative structure, the system compensates by reinforcing what is already there. The belief becomes more rigid, not because the person is committed to falsehood for its own sake, but because the belief is holding something else together.

This is one reason that conversations about conspiracy thinking often feel stuck. The two sides are addressing different problems. One side is focused on accuracy. The other is focused on stability. The first side offers facts. The second side is protecting a structure that is making life feel more tolerable. When those goals collide, facts alone are rarely enough to change the outcome.

Understanding what conspiracy thinking does does not require endorsing it. It requires recognizing that belief is not only about propositions. It is also about how people survive psychologically in environments they experience as unsafe, unpredictable, or untrustworthy. Until that is taken seriously, efforts to intervene will continue to misjudge both the persistence of these beliefs and the reactions they provoke.

This chapter is not meant to normalize conspiracy thinking as benign or acceptable. It is meant to make clear why it is so resilient. When belief is carrying emotional, social, and identity weight, it cannot be treated as a simple error to be fixed. It has become part of a broader system of psychological regulation.

The next step, then, is to look more closely at how these beliefs stabilize people internally and what happens when that stabilization is threatened. That is where the question of when to challenge and when to refrain becomes not just strategic, but ethical.

CHAPTER 3
Normal Minds in Abnormal Conditions

NORMAL MINDS IN ABNORMAL CONDITIONS

Normal Minds in Abnormal Conditions

One of the most persistent myths about conspiracy thinking is that it is primarily a problem of unusual minds. The assumption is that if someone believes something implausible, then something must be wrong with their cognitive or psychological functioning. This framing is comforting because it isolates the phenomenon. It allows the rest of society to imagine that conspiracy thinking belongs to a small, defective group rather than emerging from conditions that affect large numbers of otherwise capable people. The evidence does not support that comfort, and focusing on individual defect obscures how powerfully environmental conditions shape what kinds of explanations become psychologically viable.

Many people who hold conspiracy beliefs function well in most areas of life. They work, manage households, maintain friendships, solve complex problems, and make ordinary decisions competently. Their reasoning is not globally impaired. Their judgment is not universally poor. The belief exists within an otherwise intact psychological system. That fact alone should shift how the problem is understood, because it points away from rare pathology and toward ordinary minds operating under extraordinary informational and social pressures.

What often changes is not the mind, but the environment the mind is trying to operate within. Modern informational conditions are profoundly different from those that shaped earlier models of belief formation. People are exposed to massive volumes of contradictory claims, expert disagreement, real institutional failures, and rapidly changing narratives. The result is not simply misinformation. It is a breakdown in how people decide what is trustworthy. The usual markers of credibility become harder to rely on. Authority feels politicized. Expertise feels contested. Consensus feels unstable. In that context, the ordinary tools people use to judge what is reliable begin to fail.

When those tools fail, people do not stop needing explanations. They still need to decide what is real, who can be trusted, and how to interpret events that affect their lives. Conspiracy narratives step into that gap as a culturally available meaning system. They offer a ready-made way to organize confusion when traditional sources of authority and trust feel unreliable. The belief system supplies coherence where institutional narratives no longer feel coherent, and it does so in a way that feels emotionally and morally interpretable.

Threat saturation plays a similar role. Many people live under conditions of chronic uncertainty, whether economic, political, medical, or social. The stress is not always acute, but it is persistent. The sense that something bad could happen, that systems are fragile, and that institutions may not protect them becomes part of the background of daily life. Under those conditions, the mind becomes more oriented toward threat detection and less tolerant of ambiguity. This does not make people irrational. It makes them adaptive to perceived danger in a way that prioritizes clarity and perceived safety over probabilistic nuance.

When uncertainty and threat are chronic, people are more likely to gravitate toward explanations that feel complete and decisive. Probabilistic, nuanced accounts feel weak in comparison because they leave too much unresolved. Conspiracy narratives, by contrast, offer clarity. They identify causes. They name agents. They provide a storyline that turns diffuse unease into something concrete. Even when false, that clarity can feel preferable to ongoing ambiguity, because it reduces the psychological burden of not knowing what is happening or who is responsible.

Life transitions often intensify these dynamics. Retirement, serious illness, job loss, divorce, widowhood, relocation, and sudden shifts in social standing can destabilize a person's internal narrative. Roles that once organized identity and daily meaning may weaken or disappear. During these periods, people are not only dealing with practical disruption. They are also dealing with narrative disruption. The question of who they are, what they are for, and how they fit into the world becomes less settled. In those moments, explanatory systems that offer renewed structure, purpose, and interpretive authority can become especially appealing.

In this sense, conspiracy uptake is sometimes phase-related rather than trait-based. It may intensify during periods of loss, dislocation, or identity transition and soften when new roles and sources of stability emerge. This does not mean belief is temporary or superficial. It means that belief can become particularly attractive at moments when people are renegotiating their place in the world and searching for narratives that restore coherence and agency.

Institutional distrust further amplifies this process. When people believe that governments, corporations, media organizations, or other authorities routinely lie, conceal information, or act in self-interest, skepticism becomes a rational stance. The problem arises when skepticism slides into a generalized assumption of deception. At that point, official explanations are not just questioned. They are treated as presumptively false. Conspiracy narratives then become not an extreme alternative, but a coherent extension of lived distrust, fitting neatly into a worldview where concealment is expected rather than exceptional.

Identity pressure also matters. People do not form beliefs in a vacuum. They form them within social worlds where belonging, status, and moral alignment are at stake. In some communities, distrust of mainstream narratives is a marker of loyalty. In others, it is a marker of intelligence, independence, or moral seriousness. Holding certain beliefs becomes a way of signaling who you are and where you stand. Letting go of those beliefs can then feel like losing position, not just changing one's mind, because belief is tied to social standing and group membership.

Seen this way, conspiracy thinking is not simply a cognitive error. It is a culturally available way of making meaning under abnormal conditions. It draws on widely shared narratives of corruption, secrecy, and betrayal. It resonates with real historical examples of institutional wrongdoing. It offers a way to connect personal experience of instability with a larger explanatory framework. The belief feels less like a strange aberration and more like a plausible response within a particular interpretive environment, even when the specific claims are demonstrably false.

This is where it becomes important to address the question of mental illness directly, because it is so often misunderstood and misapplied. In most cases, conspiracy belief is not psychosis or severe mental disorder. People who are psychotic typically show a broader breakdown in reality testing. Their beliefs are not confined to a narrow ideological domain. They are often accompanied by hallucinations, disorganized thought, or significant functional decline. By contrast, many conspiracy believers show compartmentalization. They can think flexibly and pragmatically in most areas while holding rigid, implausible views in a specific informational or ideological space.

Compartmentalization is a normal psychological capacity. People routinely separate domains of thought and apply different standards of evidence and emotional investment across them. The presence of a strongly held false belief does not, by itself, indicate a global impairment. It indicates that this particular narrative has taken on special psychological meaning and protection within that person's internal system.

The distinction between ego-syntonic and ego-dystonic experience also matters. In many clinical conditions, intrusive thoughts are experienced as unwanted and distressing. The person is troubled by their own thinking and wants relief from it. In conspiracy belief, the narrative is often experienced as consistent with the person's self-concept. It fits with how they see themselves as discerning, skeptical, or morally aware. The belief is not experienced as an alien intrusion. It is experienced as an expression of who they are, which changes the motivational landscape around change.

That difference alters how challenge is experienced. When a thought is experienced as intrusive, people are often motivated to question it. When a belief is experienced as identity-consistent, people are motivated to defend it. Treating conspiracy belief as if it were simply an intrusive symptom misreads that dynamic and leads to strategies that feel invalidating rather than helpful.

Over-pathologizing also carries social and ethical risks. When conspiracy thinking is framed as mental illness, it becomes easier to dismiss, contain, or control rather than understand. It allows institutions and communities to avoid examining the conditions that make these beliefs attractive in the first place. It shifts responsibility away from broken trust, unstable systems, and chronic uncertainty and places it entirely on supposedly defective individuals. That framing may feel efficient, but it is inaccurate and ultimately counterproductive, because it undermines engagement and increases stigma while leaving the underlying drivers untouched.

Understanding conspiracy belief as a response of normal minds in abnormal conditions does not excuse harm or validate falsehood. It does, however, make clear why these beliefs are widespread, resilient, and resistant to simple correction. They are not just mistakes. They are adaptations to environments that feel untrustworthy, overwhelming, and threatening. That recognition shifts the ethical and practical terrain, because it shows that changing belief requires more than better arguments. It requires attention to the conditions that make those beliefs useful in the first place.

Without addressing those conditions, correction efforts will continue to collide with the deeper functions the beliefs are serving. The next chapter turns to one of those deeper forces directly. It examines how emotion, particularly threat, shame, loss, and meaning disruption, shapes belief and how conspiracy narratives become containers for distress that has few other places to go.

THE EMOTIONAL ECONOMY OF BELIEF

CHAPTER 4
The Emotional Economy of Belief

THE EMOTIONAL ECONOMY OF BELIEF

The Emotional Economy of Belief

Conspiracy beliefs do not exist only at the level of ideas. They are embedded in emotional systems that help people regulate threat, protect dignity, and contain experiences that would otherwise feel overwhelming. For many people, these beliefs become part of how emotional equilibrium is maintained, especially when external circumstances repeatedly signal loss of control, loss of status, or loss of safety.

Threat is one of the most powerful emotional drivers. When people feel endangered, whether physically, economically, socially, or symbolically, the mind becomes more oriented toward detecting cause and assigning responsibility. Unexplained harm is harder to tolerate than harm with an agent attached to it. A conspiracy narrative supplies that agent. It converts diffuse threat into intentional threat. Someone is doing this. Someone is responsible. That shift does not make the situation safer, but it makes it more intelligible, and intelligibility itself is emotionally regulating.

This process is closely tied to how shame and humiliation are managed. Many conspiracy narratives protect the believer from the emotional burden of feeling fooled, weak, or subordinate. If powerful forces are manipulating events, then personal failure can be reframed as victimization. The problem is not that I was naïve, incompetent, or powerless. The problem is that others are corrupt, deceptive, or malicious. That reframing preserves self-respect in situations where acknowledging error or vulnerability would feel like an intolerable loss of face.

Loss of status plays a similar role. When people experience downward mobility, diminished influence, or cultural marginalization, conspiracy narratives offer a way to interpret that loss as imposed rather than deserved. The story becomes one of sabotage rather than decline. This is not simply denial. It is an emotional strategy for preserving a coherent sense of self-worth in environments where traditional markers of success and recognition may no longer be accessible.

These emotional pressures are especially pronounced during major life transitions. Retirement, serious illness, job loss, divorce, widowhood, relocation, or sudden changes in social standing can all destabilize a person's internal narrative.

Roles that once organized daily life and identity may disappear or weaken. In these periods, people are not only dealing with practical loss. They are also dealing with narrative disruption. The question of who they are, what they are for, and where they belong becomes less clear. Conspiracy narratives can fill that gap by providing a new organizing story that restores a sense of position, purpose, and interpretive authority.

Grief and betrayal are also frequently organized through conspiracy narratives. When institutions, leaders, or systems that people trusted appear to fail them, the emotional impact is not just disappointment. It is often experienced as betrayal. Betrayal is a relational injury. It carries anger, sadness, and disorientation. A conspiracy story provides a framework for holding that injury. It gives it a cause. It gives it a target. It turns a painful relational rupture into a moral narrative with villains and victims.

In this way, belief becomes a container for distress. Fear, shame, anger, grief, and humiliation are not held as separate emotional experiences. They are bundled into a single explanatory system. The belief does not remove the distress, but it organizes it in a way that feels more manageable. The person now has a story that explains why they feel the way they do. That story gives emotional coherence to experiences that would otherwise feel chaotic or overwhelming.

There is another emotional function that is often overlooked. For some people, conspiracy narratives are not only about fear and loss. They are also about stimulation, meaning, and emotional intensity. In lives that feel flattened, repetitive, or stripped of significance, these narratives provide drama, moral clarity, and a sense of being part of a consequential story. The belief system supplies a world in which things matter, hidden forces are at work, and the believer occupies a meaningful interpretive role. This can be emotionally engaging even when it is emotionally costly. The narrative provides structure, momentum, and a sense of relevance that may be missing elsewhere.

This emotional bundling is one reason belief can become resistant to change. Challenging the belief is not just challenging an idea. It is challenging the container that is holding multiple emotional experiences at once. If the belief were to collapse, those emotions would not disappear. They would become uncontained. For many people, that prospect feels worse than maintaining a flawed narrative.

This also helps explain why emotional intensity often spikes when conspiracy beliefs are challenged. The challenge is experienced not only as intellectual disagreement, but as a threat to the emotional system that has been managing distress, identity disruption, and meaning at the same time. What appears from the outside as overreaction often reflects the destabilization of something that has been doing quiet psychological work in the background.

The emotional economy of belief also explains why people may cling to narratives that increase fear while still finding them stabilizing. A frightening story with clear villains can feel more tolerable than a vague sense of danger with no clear source. The fear is now organized. It has a shape. It has a direction. Even when that direction is misguided, it gives the emotional system something to orient around.

None of this means that emotional drivers make beliefs immune to change. It does mean that belief change is rarely just a matter of better information. It is also a matter of whether the emotional functions of the belief can be met in other ways. If fear, shame, grief, loss of status, identity disruption, and meaning hunger have no alternative containers, then the belief will continue to be needed, regardless of its accuracy.

This chapter is not an argument that emotion excuses falsehood. It is an argument that belief is often doing emotional labor that goes unseen in purely cognitive models. Until that labor is acknowledged, attempts to change belief will continue to collide with forces that are not primarily about evidence or logic.

The next chapter turns to how these emotional and narrative functions become embedded in social roles and group identities. At that point, belief is no longer just personal. It becomes a way of locating oneself in a social and moral world, which raises the stakes of change even further.

CHAPTER 5
Identity, Role, and Belonging

Identity, Role, and Belonging

Conspiracy thinking rarely remains a private cognitive position. Over time, it often becomes a way of locating oneself in a social and moral landscape. The belief is not only something a person holds. It becomes something a person is. It supplies a role, a stance, and a sense of placement in relation to others. Once belief is serving that function, changing it no longer means updating an opinion. It means relinquishing a social position.

For many people, conspiracy narratives offer a ready-made identity: the person who sees through deception, who is not fooled by appearances, who understands what others are blind to. This identity carries moral weight. It positions the believer as vigilant rather than naïve, courageous rather than compliant, perceptive rather than manipulated. These are not neutral traits. They are values. They allow the person to see themselves as occupying a morally and intellectually elevated position in a world they no longer trust.

This role can be especially compelling for people who feel that other avenues for recognition, status, or influence have narrowed. When occupational authority, social standing, or cultural relevance decline, conspiracy thinking can provide an alternative source of significance. The person may no longer be central in their workplace, community, or family system, but they can still be central in an interpretive role. They become the one who knows. They become the one who warns. They become the one who is not fooled. That role can partially substitute for lost forms of status and authority.

Belonging also plays a powerful role. Conspiracy communities, whether online or offline, offer shared language, shared narratives, and shared moral boundaries. They define who is awake and who is asleep, who can be trusted and who cannot, who is inside and who is outside. These boundaries do social work. They create a sense of group identity and provide a framework for loyalty and mutual validation. Disagreement from outsiders is not just disagreement. It is often reinterpreted as evidence of corruption, manipulation, or complicity.

Once belief becomes tied to belonging, the cost of doubt rises sharply. Letting go of the belief is no longer just an internal process. It can mean risking exclusion, ridicule, or loss of community. For some people, especially those who are socially isolated in other parts of their lives, conspiracy communities may represent one of the few places where they feel understood, respected, or taken seriously. In that context, belief is not just an idea. It is a ticket to connection.

The role of legitimate grievance complicates this picture in important ways. History provides real examples of institutional betrayal, cover-ups, and abuses of power. Watergate, COINTELPRO, the Tuskegee experiments, financial scandals, and documented intelligence operations all make it clear that conspiracy is not a purely imaginary phenomenon. For many individuals and communities, distrust is not a personality trait. It is a learned response to real experience.

When people have been lied to, marginalized, exploited, or dismissed by powerful institutions, suspicion does not arise in a vacuum. It is shaped by memory, culture, and collective history. In those contexts, conspiracy narratives can feel morally justified. They resonate with past experience. They align with a sense that official stories cannot be taken at face value. This does not make all conspiracy beliefs accurate, but it does mean that the emotional and moral logic behind them is not always irrational.

This is one reason why attempts to treat conspiracy thinking as mere gullibility or pathology often fail. For some people, belief is intertwined with a broader story about injustice, betrayal, and unaccountable power. Challenging the belief without acknowledging that history can feel like a second betrayal. It can sound like a demand to trust systems that have already proven untrustworthy. In that sense, belief can become a form of moral protest as well as an explanatory system.

Role replacement is another key dynamic. When people lose socially valued roles, whether through retirement, unemployment, illness, or cultural displacement, they often search for new ways to define their contribution and relevance. Conspiracy thinking can supply a replacement role that is immediately available and emotionally potent. The person becomes a researcher, a watchdog, a truth-teller, or a defender against hidden threats. These roles offer purpose and a sense of ongoing mission.

Once a person is embedded in that role, belief maintenance becomes part of role maintenance. Letting go of the belief would not only change what the person thinks. It would change who they are allowed to be in their own narrative. It would require finding a different way to feel competent, significant, and morally positioned. That is a much larger psychological shift than simply changing one's mind.

Evangelizing behavior often reflects this role investment. Sharing information, warning others, and correcting perceived deception reinforce the person's identity as someone who knows and who cares. Each interaction becomes a performance of the role. Pushback from others can even strengthen it, because resistance confirms the narrative that truth is being suppressed and that the role is necessary.

This helps explain why some people appear more energized by conflict around their beliefs than by quiet agreement. The conflict itself reinforces identity. It confirms the person's self-concept as someone who stands apart, who is willing to be unpopular, and who is willing to fight for what they see as truth. In this way, opposition becomes part of the emotional and identity economy of belief.

None of this means that people consciously choose these roles in a calculated way. In most cases, the shift happens gradually. Belief leads to engagement. Engagement leads to community. Community leads to role. Over time, the belief becomes embedded in how the person understands themselves in relation to others. At that point, belief change is no longer just an intellectual adjustment. It is a social and identity transition.

This chapter is not an argument that identity and belonging make beliefs true. It is an argument that identity and belonging make beliefs durable. They raise the psychological and social costs of change. They turn disagreement into something that feels like a personal and moral challenge. Without addressing those layers, attempts to change belief are likely to feel like attempts to erase a person's place in the world.

The next chapter turns to how these beliefs are actively maintained over time through attention, repetition, social reinforcement, and feedback loops. At that stage, belief is not only emotionally and socially supported. It becomes structurally reinforced in ways that make disengagement even more difficult.

How These Beliefs Are Maintained

CHAPTER 6

How These Beliefs Are Maintained

How These Beliefs Are Maintained

How These Beliefs Are Maintained

Once conspiracy beliefs become emotionally useful and identity-relevant, they do not persist by accident. They are actively maintained through a set of psychological, social, and technological processes that make the beliefs easier to rehearse, harder to dislodge, and more resistant to challenge. These processes operate quietly, often outside of conscious awareness, and together they create a system that favors continuity over revision.

One of the most powerful maintenance mechanisms is narrative rehearsal. People return to the same stories repeatedly, retelling them to themselves and to others. Each repetition strengthens familiarity and fluency. The narrative becomes easier to recall and easier to explain. Over time, familiarity can be mistaken for truth. The story feels right not because it has been tested and confirmed, but because it has been told so many times that it has become the default frame through which new information is interpreted.

Selective attention reinforces this effect. Once a narrative is established, people become more likely to notice information that fits it and to overlook or discount information that does not. This is not unique to conspiracy thinking. It is a general feature of human cognition. What makes conspiracy narratives different is that they often include built-in explanations for why disconfirming evidence should be ignored. Contradiction is reframed as deception. Silence is reframed as suppression. Lack of proof is reframed as proof of how well the conspiracy is hidden. The narrative thus protects itself from falsification by redefining what counts as evidence.

Social reinforcement adds another layer. Beliefs are echoed, affirmed, and elaborated within communities that share the same narrative. Agreement is rewarded with validation. Doubt may be met with suspicion or subtle social cost. Over time, the group becomes a primary reference point for what is considered credible. The person is no longer evaluating claims in isolation. They are evaluating how those claims fit within a shared reality that is constantly being reinforced by others.

Technology intensifies these dynamics. Algorithmic systems are designed to

How These Beliefs Are Maintained

maximize engagement, not accuracy. Content that provokes strong emotional responses is more likely to be surfaced, shared, and repeated. Conspiracy narratives often carry high emotional charge, which makes them well suited to this environment. As people interact with such content, they are shown more of it. The informational environment becomes increasingly narrow, giving the impression that the belief is widely supported and constantly confirmed.

This creates the illusion of consensus. When most of what someone sees aligns with their narrative, it becomes harder to imagine that alternative interpretations are credible or common. The belief feels socially validated, even if it remains a minority view in the broader population. That perceived validation strengthens confidence and reduces motivation to seek out or trust dissenting sources.

Identity-threat feedback loops further lock beliefs in place. When a belief is challenged, the challenge is often experienced not just as disagreement, but as a threat to the person's role, status, or moral standing. That threat activates defensive responses. The person becomes more motivated to protect the narrative, to seek confirming information, and to distance themselves from sources of challenge. The act of being challenged thus strengthens the very processes that maintain the belief.

Over time, these mechanisms create a self-sustaining system. The belief is rehearsed, selectively supported, socially validated, technologically amplified, and defended as part of identity. Each element reinforces the others. The result is a closed loop in which revision becomes increasingly difficult, not because the person is incapable of change, but because change would require disrupting multiple interconnected supports at once.

It is in this context that conspiracy thinking is sometimes mistakenly described as obsessional. The repetition, preoccupation, and rigidity can resemble features of obsessive thinking. But the underlying structure is different. Obsessive thoughts are typically experienced as intrusive and unwanted. The person tries to resist them. They are distressing in and of themselves. In conspiracy thinking, the narrative is usually chosen, valued, and defended. The person may be distressed by what they believe, but the belief itself is not experienced as alien. It is experienced as meaningful and identity-consistent.

This difference matters for how persistence is understood. In obsession, repetition is driven by anxiety relief through compulsion. In conspiracy thinking, repetition is driven by commitment, identity reinforcement, and social signaling. The person is not trying to get rid of the thought. They are trying to live inside it, share it, and organize around it. The emotional payoff is not only relief from anxiety, but reinforcement of role, belonging, and moral position.

There are cases where obsessive features coexist with conspiracy thinking. Some individuals show high levels of rumination, checking behavior, or compulsive consumption of related content. In those situations, clinical assessment is appropriate. But even then, the presence of obsessive traits does not fully explain the belief system. The narrative usually still carries identity, emotional, and social functions that go beyond anxiety-driven compulsion.

Understanding maintenance processes changes how persistence is interpreted. What looks like stubbornness is often the product of a system that is doing exactly what it was shaped to do. It is protecting coherence, belonging, and emotional stability. Breaking into that system with facts alone is unlikely to succeed, because facts address only one layer of a much larger structure.

This is why repeated correction so often leads to fatigue and frustration on both sides. The person offering correction feels unheard. The person receiving it feels attacked or misunderstood. Both are responding to different parts of the system. Without recognizing the maintenance mechanisms at work, each side misreads the other's behavior and attributes it to bad faith, stupidity, or malice.

The next chapter turns to a different but related issue. Even when the psychological dynamics are understood, ethical questions remain. The needs of individuals and the needs of society do not always align. The same belief that stabilizes one person can create harm for others. Navigating that tension requires separating two ethical domains that are often confused.

Two Ethical Domains

CHAPTER 7

Two Ethical Domains

Two Ethical Domains

Two Ethical Domains

Conversations about conspiracy thinking often collapse two very different ethical questions into one. The first concerns the well-being of the individual who holds the belief. The second concerns the potential harm that belief may cause to others and to society more broadly. When these two domains are treated as interchangeable, responses become confused, inconsistent, and morally overextended.

From a clinical and relational perspective, the primary ethical question is what helps this person function, cope, and remain psychologically intact. The focus is on emotional safety, dignity, and the preservation of relationships where possible. The goal is not immediate correctness. It is stability, trust, and the capacity for reflective thought. In this domain, restraint, timing, and indirect approaches may be not only appropriate but necessary.

From a public-health and societal perspective, the ethical question is different. The focus is on preventing harm, reducing risk, and protecting others from the downstream effects of false or dangerous beliefs. Here, the priority is not the comfort of the individual believer. It is the safety of vulnerable populations, the integrity of shared systems, and the prevention of violence, exploitation, or widespread harm. In this domain, tolerance for falsehood is lower and intervention thresholds are different.

These two ethical domains operate under different principles. What is compassionate and appropriate in one domain may be insufficient or irresponsible in the other. A clinician may prioritize maintaining a therapeutic alliance even when a belief is false. A public institution may have a duty to counter that same belief aggressively if it undermines public safety. Confusion arises when people assume that one ethical stance should automatically govern all contexts.

This role confusion leads to moral overreach. Family members may feel obligated to act like public health officials in private relationships. Clinicians may feel pressure to become enforcers of societal norms rather than caretakers of individual well-being. Public commentators may frame disagreement as a moral failure rather than as a complex psychological and social process. In each case, ethical standards appropriate to one domain are misapplied to another.

The cost of this confusion is high. In personal relationships, moralized confrontation often damages trust and reduces the likelihood of any meaningful influence. In institutional settings, excessive deference to individual emotional needs can allow harmful beliefs to spread unchecked. Neither extreme serves its intended purpose when applied in the wrong context.

Separating these domains clarifies responsibility. In individual care contexts, the ethical obligation is to reduce suffering, preserve dignity, and support psychological flexibility. That does not mean endorsing falsehood. It means recognizing that immediate correction may not be the most humane or effective intervention. The aim is to create conditions under which the person can tolerate uncertainty, reflect, and potentially revise over time.

In societal contexts, the ethical obligation is to limit harm and protect others. That may require direct correction, policy enforcement, and public communication strategies that prioritize clarity over individual comfort. The aim is not to preserve every relationship. It is to reduce risk and prevent damage at scale.

Problems arise when people try to collapse these responsibilities into a single moral stance. The same language is used for private conversation and public policy. The same emotional expectations are placed on family members and on institutions. The result is frustration on all sides, because the tools that work in one domain are poorly suited to the other.

Understanding this distinction does not make ethical decisions easier. It makes them clearer. It forces a more honest assessment of what role one is playing and what obligations follow from that role. It also reduces the temptation to turn every disagreement into a moral emergency or, conversely, to treat every harmful belief as a purely personal matter.

This chapter does not argue that one domain is more important than the other. It argues that they are different and must be treated as such. The failure to separate them leads to both ineffective care and inadequate protection. Ethical clarity begins with knowing which domain you are operating in and what goals are appropriate to that context.

The next chapter addresses a related concern that often arises at this point. If restraint and timing matter in individual contexts, does that mean abandoning truth or sliding into ethical relativism. The answer is no, but explaining why requires careful distinction between restraint and endorsement.

Truth, Harm, And The Limits Of Correction

CHAPTER 8
Truth, Harm, and the Limits of Correction

Truth, Harm, And The Limits Of Correction

Truth, Harm, and the Limits of Correction

The emphasis on restraint, timing, and function can easily be misunderstood as a form of ethical relativism. If beliefs are serving psychological purposes, some conclude, then perhaps accuracy no longer matters. Perhaps truth becomes optional. That is not the argument being made here. The distinction is not between truth and comfort. It is between different ways of pursuing truth in contexts where human psychology is part of the system.

Affirming reality does not require weaponizing it. There is a difference between holding a commitment to what is true and using that commitment as a tool for domination, humiliation, or moral positioning. In many conversations about conspiracy thinking, truth is not offered as shared ground. It is wielded as a verdict. The subtext becomes not simply that a claim is wrong, but that the person is defective, foolish, or morally compromised for holding it.

That use of truth creates predictable defensive reactions. People do not experience it as clarification. They experience it as status attack. The content of the correction becomes inseparable from its social meaning. The person is not just being informed. They are being positioned as inferior. In that context, resistance is not a rejection of reality. It is a rejection of humiliation.

The ethical distinction, then, is between endorsement and restraint. Restraint does not mean agreeing with falsehood. It means choosing not to force correction in ways that are likely to produce greater harm, entrenchment, or relational rupture. It means recognizing that immediate confrontation is not always the most responsible way to serve truth, especially when it predictably reduces the likelihood of any future openness.

Timing and sequencing matter because psychological systems change over time. A person who cannot tolerate uncertainty or loss in one phase of life may be able to tolerate it later. A belief that feels essential in a moment of crisis may become less necessary when stability returns. Ethical engagement takes these temporal dynamics seriously. It asks not only whether something is true, but whether this is the moment and the method that make truth receivable.

Truth, Harm, And The Limits Of Correction

Restraint is sometimes protective. It can preserve relationships that serve as future channels for influence. It can prevent escalation that hardens identity and increases harm. It can allow space for emotional processing that makes later reflection possible. In that sense, restraint is not passivity. It is a strategic and ethical choice grounded in an understanding of human psychology.

This differs from appeasement or denial of harm. Appeasement involves accepting falsehood in order to avoid conflict. Denial involves minimizing the real-world consequences of belief. Restraint, as used here, involves maintaining clarity about what is true while choosing not to engage in forms of correction that are likely to worsen the situation. It is an active posture, not a surrender of standards.

The moral tension arises because truth has social consequences. How it is delivered, when it is delivered, and by whom it is delivered all affect how it is received. Ethical practice requires attention to those factors, not because truth is fragile, but because people are. Ignoring that reality does not make one more principled. It often makes one less effective and, in some cases, more harmful.

This does not mean that all beliefs should be treated gently or indefinitely tolerated. Some beliefs create direct risk. Some enable coercion, abuse, or violence. Some undermine basic safety. In those situations, restraint is no longer protective. It becomes complicity. Ethical responsibility shifts, and intervention becomes necessary regardless of the individual's psychological comfort.

Understanding the limits of correction is therefore not a way of avoiding hard choices. It is a way of making those choices more consciously. It replaces moral reflex with ethical judgment. It asks what serves truth and reduces harm in this specific context, with this specific person, under these specific conditions.

The next chapter addresses situations where neutrality is not an option. There are cases in which harm, risk, or exploitation override considerations of timing and emotional readiness. In those cases, protective confrontation is not only justified. It is ethically required.

CHAPTER 9

When Harm Requires Intervention

WHEN HARM REQUIRES INTERVENTION

When Harm Requires Intervention

Not all contexts allow for restraint. While many conspiracy beliefs primarily affect the believer and their immediate relationships, some beliefs create clear and unacceptable risk to others. In those situations, the ethical priority shifts. The question is no longer primarily about preserving psychological stability or relational connection. It becomes about preventing harm, protecting vulnerable people, and interrupting trajectories that could lead to serious damage.

Medical danger is one of the most obvious non-neutral situations. Beliefs that lead someone to refuse lifesaving treatment, reject basic medical care for themselves or their dependents, or follow dangerous health practices cross a threshold. At that point, the belief is no longer a private meaning system. It becomes a mechanism of physical risk. Ethical responsibility requires intervention that prioritizes safety, even if it destabilizes the belief system or strains the relationship.

Coercion and abuse represent another clear boundary. When conspiracy narratives are used to justify controlling behavior, isolation of family members, manipulation of partners, or punishment of children, the belief becomes part of a harmful power structure. In these cases, psychological function for the believer cannot outweigh the rights and safety of others. The narrative is no longer just explanatory. It is being used instrumentally to dominate, intimidate, or restrict autonomy. Intervention is not optional in these circumstances. It is an ethical obligation.

Violence and incitement mark an even more urgent threshold. When beliefs include calls for violent action, endorsement of harm to specific groups, or encouragement of vigilantism, the system has moved beyond psychological coping into direct threat. At that point, protective confrontation is required, even if it escalates conflict. The goal shifts from persuasion to prevention. The ethical priority is to reduce immediate risk, not to preserve the internal coherence of the belief.

Severe functional impairment also changes the calculus. When conspiracy thinking consumes so much psychological and behavioral space that a person can no longer work, maintain basic relationships, care for themselves, or engage in ordinary life tasks, the belief has become a source of disability. In those cases, the belief is no longer simply stabilizing. It is actively destabilizing. Clinical intervention may be appropriate, not because the belief is false, but because the person's ability to function has been significantly compromised.

In all of these situations, neutrality is not an ethical stance. Silence, avoidance, or purely indirect engagement can function as tacit permission for harm to continue. The responsibility to protect others and prevent damage overrides the goal of preserving emotional equilibrium for the believer. This does not mean that intervention should be cruel, humiliating, or reckless. It does mean that safety takes precedence over comfort.

Protective confrontation is different from moralized attack. The goal is not to win an argument or assert superiority. The goal is to interrupt a harmful trajectory. That may involve setting firm boundaries, involving external authorities, or mobilizing institutional supports. It may require clear statements about unacceptable behavior. It may require prioritizing the needs of those at risk over the preferences of the believer.

These situations also reveal why simplistic models of persuasion fail. When harm is present, the ethical task is not to gently guide belief change over time. It is to act in the present to reduce risk. That may or may not result in belief revision. The primary metric is safety, not agreement.

Recognizing these thresholds helps clarify earlier chapters. Restraint is not a universal rule. It is a context-dependent strategy. When beliefs remain primarily internal and relational, restraint may be appropriate. When beliefs become vehicles for physical harm, coercion, or serious impairment, restraint becomes unethical.

This chapter draws a hard line, not to contradict the earlier emphasis on psychological function, but to place it within a broader moral framework. Psychological stability is important. It is not absolute. The well-being of others, especially those with less power, sets limits on how much accommodation is appropriate.

The next chapter moves from these boundary conditions to a more nuanced and difficult task. It offers a framework for deciding when to challenge and when not to in the many situations that fall between clear harm and purely private belief. This is the chapter where psychological judgment becomes most central.

When To Challenge And When Not To

CHAPTER 10
When to Challenge and When Not To

When To Challenge And When Not To

When to Challenge and When Not To

Most real-world situations involving conspiracy thinking do not fall neatly into categories of harmless belief or clear, immediate danger. They exist in a middle terrain where the ethical, relational, and psychological factors are mixed. In this terrain, the question is not simply whether a belief is true or false. The question is whether challenging it in this moment, in this way, with this person, is likely to reduce harm or increase it.

Effective judgment begins with functional assessment. The first task is to understand what the belief is doing for the person. Is it stabilizing them emotionally. Is it organizing fear or grief. Is it providing identity, purpose, or belonging. Is it compensating for loss of status, trust, or control. A belief that is carrying significant emotional or identity load will be harder to loosen and more costly to remove. Challenging such a belief without recognizing its function is more likely to provoke defense than reflection.

Emotional and situational load matters as much as content. A person under acute stress, loss, illness, or major life disruption has fewer psychological resources available for tolerating uncertainty and self-questioning. In those states, belief functions as a scaffold. Removing it increases instability. The same person, in a calmer and more supported phase of life, may be far more capable of holding ambiguity and revising narratives. Timing is not a technical detail. It is central to whether challenge can be metabolized or whether it will be experienced as threat.

Identity binding is another key factor. The more tightly a belief is woven into how a person understands who they are, the more threatening direct challenge will feel. If the belief supports a role such as truth-teller, protector, or moral resister, then challenge is not just disagreement. It is an implicit threat to dignity and self-concept. In those cases, attacking the belief often strengthens it by activating identity defense. A more effective approach may involve engaging the values behind the identity rather than the narrative itself.

Relationship security also shapes what is possible. In relationships marked by trust, respect, and emotional safety, people are more willing to tolerate disagreement and self-doubt. In relationships marked by contempt, power struggle, or repeated humiliation, challenge is more likely to be interpreted as attack. The same words can land very differently depending on whether the relationship feels secure or adversarial. Without sufficient relational safety, even accurate correction can function as a threat.

Status and face threat further complicate challenge. Being publicly corrected, contradicted, or exposed can trigger powerful shame responses. When people feel that their competence, intelligence, or moral standing is being questioned in front of others, defense becomes almost automatic. In those situations, the cost of being wrong is not just cognitive. It is social and emotional. Strategic restraint may involve shifting difficult conversations into private contexts or lowering the public stakes so that reflection becomes possible without humiliation.

Substitution capacity is often overlooked. If a belief is removed, what will take its place. If the belief is providing coherence, agency, or meaning, and there is no alternative structure available, the system will resist change. Challenge is more likely to succeed when there are other sources of meaning, belonging, or agency that can absorb the functions the belief has been serving. Without substitution, challenge creates a vacuum that the old belief is likely to rush back in to fill.

Psychological flexibility is another critical variable. Some people can hold multiple perspectives, tolerate ambivalence, and revise narratives without feeling that their identity is at stake. Others experience belief as all-or-nothing. Inflexible systems treat doubt as betrayal and complexity as weakness. In those systems, direct challenge is more likely to be experienced as existential threat. The goal in such cases may not be immediate belief change, but gradual expansion of tolerance for uncertainty and mixed evidence.

Taken together, these factors help identify indicators for thoughtful challenge. Challenge is more likely to be constructive when the belief is not tightly bound to identity, when emotional load is manageable, when relationship security is strong, when the social stakes are low, when alternative sources of meaning exist, and when the person shows some capacity for flexibility and reflection. In those conditions, gentle, curious, and collaborative challenge may open space for revision rather than triggering defense.

There are also indicators for strategic restraint. When belief is deeply identity-bound, when the person is under acute stress, when the relationship is fragile, when public humiliation is likely, when no alternative supports are available, and when rigidity is high, restraint may be the more responsible choice. Restraint does not mean agreement. It means choosing not to force a confrontation that is unlikely to produce benefit and is likely to increase entrenchment or relational damage.

Indirect engagement often becomes the most effective tool in these cases. Rather than arguing about the belief itself, one can focus on strengthening alternative identities, restoring agency in other areas, reducing isolation, or addressing the underlying losses that made the belief necessary. Conversations can center on shared values, practical goals, or emotional experiences rather than on contested narratives. Over time, these shifts can weaken the psychological grip of the belief without triggering direct defense.

Ethical boundaries remain essential. Strategic restraint is not unlimited tolerance. It is bounded by the risk of harm, coercion, or severe impairment discussed in earlier chapters. The framework offered here is not a way to avoid difficult conversations forever. It is a way to decide when those conversations are likely to help and when they are likely to harm.

Redefining success is part of this framework. Success is not always belief change. In many cases, success looks like reduced rigidity, decreased preoccupation, greater tolerance for ambiguity, improved relationships, or less emotional volatility around the belief. These shifts may not produce public renunciation of a narrative, but they can meaningfully reduce harm and increase psychological flexibility. In the long run, those changes create conditions under which deeper belief revision becomes possible.

This chapter does not offer a formula. It offers a way of thinking that replaces moral reflex with psychological judgment. It asks for attention to function, timing, identity, relationship, and capacity. It treats belief not as a static error, but as part of a living psychological system. Working with that system requires discernment, not just certainty.

The next chapter turns to practical ways of weakening the grip of conspiracy beliefs without direct confrontation. These indirect interventions often do more to reduce the need for the belief than any argument ever could.

CHAPTER 11
Indirect Interventions

Indirect Interventions

Indirect Interventions

Directly attacking a conspiracy belief is often the least effective way to weaken it. When belief is serving emotional, identity, and social functions, confrontation tends to strengthen the very structures that keep it in place. Indirect interventions work differently. Rather than targeting the narrative head-on, they reduce the conditions that make the narrative necessary. Over time, this can loosen the grip of the belief without triggering the defensive systems that direct challenge so often activates.

One of the most powerful indirect strategies is strengthening alternative identities. When a person's sense of self becomes narrowly defined around being a truth-teller, resister, or outsider, the belief carries disproportionate psychological weight. Expanding identity gives the person other ways to experience competence, dignity, and purpose. This can involve supporting roles related to work, caregiving, creativity, community involvement, or skill development. When identity is more distributed, no single belief has to carry the full load of self-definition.

Restoring agency in concrete areas of life is another key lever. Many conspiracy beliefs flourish in environments where people feel acted upon rather than acting. Supporting experiences where the person can make meaningful choices, solve real problems, and see the impact of their actions can reduce the emotional need for grand explanatory narratives. Agency at a local, tangible level often does more to stabilize people than abstract explanations about distant systems.

Reducing isolation also matters. Social isolation amplifies rumination, narrows informational input, and strengthens identification with online or ideologically homogeneous communities. Increasing access to varied, real-world relationships can introduce alternative perspectives without direct argument. It also provides emotional regulation that does not depend on shared narratives of threat and betrayal. Belonging that is not contingent on belief reduces the social cost of doubt.

Addressing underlying losses is often central. Many people who become deeply invested in conspiracy narratives have experienced losses of status, security, trust, or meaning. Those losses may be economic, relational, cultural, or existential. When these experiences are acknowledged and worked through, the belief no longer has to do as much emotional work. Grief that is named and supported is less likely to require a villain to contain it.

Modeling uncertainty tolerance is another indirect but powerful intervention. When people see respected others openly hold complexity, revise views, and tolerate ambiguity without humiliation, it creates a template for how doubt can be survivable. This is especially important in environments where certainty is treated as strength and ambivalence as weakness. Demonstrating that one can remain grounded, respected, and competent while saying "I don't know" reduces the psychological cost of not having a complete narrative.

Value-based alignment can also open space. Rather than arguing about specific claims, conversations can focus on shared values such as safety, fairness, protecting children, or personal freedom. When those values are acknowledged and respected, it becomes possible to explore whether particular narratives actually serve those values. This reframing shifts the conversation from who is right to what matters, which can lower defensiveness and invite reflection.

Indirect interventions are not passive. They require patience, attentiveness, and a willingness to work at levels that do not produce immediate visible change. They also require realistic expectations. Weakening the psychological need for a belief is often a slow process. It involves altering emotional, social, and identity conditions over time rather than delivering a decisive argument.

At this point, it is important to address a factor that is rarely discussed but often decisive: the emotional reactions of the people trying to help. Family members, clinicians, friends, and concerned professionals do not enter these interactions as neutral observers. They bring their own emotional responses, many of which are understandable but can quietly undermine indirect work if they go unexamined.

Moral disgust is one of the most common. Hearing beliefs that feel dangerous, offensive, or irrational can trigger a visceral sense of revulsion or contempt. Even when unspoken, this emotional stance is often communicated through tone, facial expression, or subtle distancing. The other person senses being judged, which increases shame and defensiveness and strengthens identity-based protection of the belief.

Fatigue is another frequent factor. Long-term exposure to rigid beliefs, repeated arguments, and lack of visible progress can wear people down. When fatigue sets in, helpers may become curt, impatient, or disengaged. The interaction shifts from curiosity and containment to endurance and resentment. This emotional shift often narrows the relational space in which indirect change can occur.

A sense of superiority can also emerge, sometimes in subtle forms. Helpers may begin to see themselves as the rational ones dealing with someone who is confused, gullible, or morally compromised. Even when factually grounded, this stance changes the relational dynamic. It turns the interaction into a hierarchy rather than a collaboration. That hierarchy is often experienced by the believer as humiliation, which strengthens rather than weakens the psychological need for the belief.

The desire to win is another powerful and often unrecognized driver. Helpers may become invested in proving a point, correcting an error, or achieving visible acknowledgment of being right. This is understandable in a culture that rewards debate and correction. But when winning becomes a primary emotional goal, the interaction shifts away from reducing belief load and toward defending status. The conversation becomes a contest rather than a process, and the belief becomes something to defend rather than something to reconsider.

Fear also plays a role for helpers. Fear of harm, fear of radicalization, fear of losing the relationship, or fear of being complicit can all intensify urgency. That urgency can translate into pressure, repeated confrontation, or escalating stakes. While motivated by care, it often communicates threat rather than safety, which activates the very systems that keep belief rigid.

Indirect work requires helpers to regulate their own emotional systems as much as they engage the other person's. This does not mean suppressing concern or pretending that harmful beliefs are acceptable. It means recognizing how one's own reactions shape the psychological field of the interaction. Containment is a two-person process. If the helper is dysregulated, shaming, or status-oriented, the system becomes less safe for flexibility.

This is one reason indirect interventions are more demanding than confrontation. They require staying engaged without the immediate relief of correction. They require tolerating ambiguity about whether one is making progress. They require holding boundaries while remaining emotionally available. For many people, this is harder than stating the facts and disengaging.

The advantage is that indirect interventions work with the psychological system rather than against it. They reduce the load that the belief is carrying. When that load decreases, the belief often becomes less rigid, less central, and less emotionally charged. At that point, direct discussion may become more possible and more productive, not because someone was defeated, but because the belief is no longer needed in the same way.

This chapter does not suggest that indirect work is always sufficient. In cases of harm, coercion, or danger, earlier principles still apply. Safety and protection take priority. Indirect approaches are most appropriate when the primary goal is long-term flexibility, relationship preservation, and gradual reduction of belief centrality.

The next chapter turns to one of the most difficult practical challenges in this work. It focuses on how to preserve relationships in the presence of deep disagreement without collapsing reality or engaging in ongoing moral warfare.

CHAPTER 12
Preserving Relationships

Preserving Relationships

Deep disagreement over conspiracy beliefs places relationships under sustained strain. The disagreement is rarely confined to ideas. It often carries moral judgment, emotional injury, and questions about respect and trust. Over time, this can turn ordinary relationships into ongoing battlegrounds, where every interaction risks becoming another argument about reality itself.

Preserving relationships in this context does not mean avoiding all disagreement. It means managing disagreement in ways that do not turn it into a constant test of loyalty or intelligence. When every conversation becomes a referendum on who is right, the relationship becomes a vehicle for humiliation, defense, and scorekeeping. That dynamic rarely produces reflection. It produces entrenchment and exhaustion.

Avoiding humiliation dynamics is especially important. Public correction, sarcasm, and moralized language can quickly turn disagreement into a threat to dignity. Once someone feels shamed, the psychological system shifts from curiosity to protection. The person is no longer evaluating ideas. They are defending face. Even accurate statements become experienced as attacks, and the emotional residue of those interactions accumulates over time.

Boundary setting is often necessary, but it must be done carefully. Boundaries are not punishments. They are clarifications of what one is willing and able to engage with. Saying that certain topics are off-limits in certain settings can protect the relationship from being consumed by conflict. It also communicates that the relationship is valued for more than ideological alignment. When boundaries are framed as self-protection rather than moral judgment, they are more likely to be respected and less likely to escalate into power struggles.

Managing disagreement without rupture also involves choosing when not to pursue every point of contention. Not every false claim needs to be corrected in real time. Constant correction can transform the relationship into a monitoring system rather than a human connection. Selectivity allows space for shared experiences that are not defined by conflict. It preserves moments of normalcy that can buffer the relationship against the cumulative stress of disagreement.

In some cases, distance becomes protective. When interactions consistently escalate into hostility, withdrawal may be necessary to prevent ongoing emotional injury. Distance is not always abandonment. It can be a way of preserving what remains of a relationship by reducing exposure to cycles that reliably produce harm. This is especially true when one party uses belief as a tool for domination, provocation, or repeated boundary violation.

Preserving relationships also requires clarity about what cannot be compromised. Maintaining connection does not mean accepting coercion, abuse, or ongoing disrespect. It does not mean tolerating behavior that endangers others. Relational preservation has limits. Those limits are defined by safety, dignity, and the right to emotional integrity.

The goal in this chapter is not to offer techniques for endless accommodation. It is to articulate a stance that values connection while refusing to let disagreement become a weapon. It recognizes that relationships are not simply channels for belief change. They are ends in themselves. When relationships are preserved with integrity, they create the possibility of future influence. When they are destroyed by moral warfare, that possibility disappears.

Preserving relationships in the presence of deep disagreements about what's true is emotionally demanding. It requires tolerating unresolved tension. It requires resisting the urge to win. It requires prioritizing long-term connection over short-term satisfaction. These choices are not always possible or appropriate, but when they are, they can reduce harm and keep open channels that may matter later.

The next chapter shifts focus from relationships to outcomes. It addresses what real change actually looks like in this domain and why conversion is often the wrong metric for success.

CHAPTER 13
What Real Change Looks Like

WHAT REAL CHANGE LOOKS LIKE

What Real Change Looks Like

In most public conversations about conspiracy beliefs, change is imagined as conversion. The person is expected to renounce the belief, accept the correct explanation, and publicly acknowledge error. This model is appealing because it is clear and measurable. It offers a visible endpoint. But in practice, it is often the wrong metric for progress.

Belief systems that are emotionally, socially, and identity-bound rarely dissolve all at once. They soften. They lose centrality. They become less rigid and less consuming. The person may still hold elements of the narrative while becoming more capable of tolerating uncertainty, considering alternative explanations, or shifting attention to other areas of life. From the outside, this can look like failure. From a psychological perspective, it often represents meaningful movement.

Reduced rigidity is one of the earliest signs of change. The person becomes less defensive, less absolutist, and less reactive to disagreement. They may still disagree strongly, but they are less likely to interpret every challenge as personal attack. They show greater capacity to pause, listen, and consider without immediately needing to rebut. This flexibility is not dramatic, but it is foundational. Without it, deeper revision is unlikely.

Decreased preoccupation is another important indicator. When conspiracy narratives are no longer the dominant topic of thought, conversation, and emotional energy, the belief loses much of its psychological power. The person may still endorse parts of the narrative, but it no longer organizes their daily life. They spend less time consuming related content. They bring it up less often. Other interests and concerns begin to reclaim space.

Increased tolerance for ambivalence is also a meaningful shift. The person becomes more able to hold mixed feelings and partial uncertainty without rushing to resolve them into a single, totalizing explanation. They may say that they are not sure about certain aspects of the narrative. They may acknowledge limits to what they know. They may entertain the possibility that more than one explanation could be partially true. This tolerance for ambiguity is a major marker of psychological flexibility.

Functional coexistence is often a more realistic goal than belief elimination. The belief may persist in some form, but it no longer dictates behavior in harmful or disruptive ways. The person can maintain relationships, work effectively, and participate in ordinary life without the belief constantly intruding. From a harm-reduction perspective, this is often a significant improvement, even if it falls short of full ideological change.

These forms of change are easy to miss if conversion is the only yardstick. When observers focus exclusively on whether the person has abandoned the belief, they may overlook important psychological gains. They may conclude that nothing has changed when, in fact, the belief has lost much of its emotional and functional grip.

There is also a temporal dimension to change. Shifts often occur gradually and unevenly. People may oscillate between openness and rigidity depending on stress, life events, and social context. A person who becomes more flexible in one phase of life may become more rigid again during a crisis. This does not mean that earlier change was illusory. It reflects the dynamic nature of psychological systems responding to changing conditions.

Expecting dramatic, linear transformation sets both helpers and relationships up for frustration. It encourages premature confrontation, disappointment, and burnout. It also incentivizes performative change, where people say the right things without having done the deeper emotional and identity work that makes change durable.

Redefining success as softening rather than conversion changes how engagement is experienced. It shifts the focus from winning arguments to reducing harm and increasing flexibility. It values psychological movement even when ideological movement is incomplete. It recognizes that many of the most important changes are internal and incremental rather than public and declarative.

This does not mean that full belief change is impossible or undesirable. It means that treating it as the primary or only meaningful outcome is often unrealistic. In many cases, the conditions that made the belief necessary must change before the belief itself can fully dissolve. When those conditions improve, belief change may follow. When they do not, partial softening may be the most that is ethically and psychologically available.

Understanding what real change looks like helps recalibrate expectations. It allows people to stay engaged without demanding impossible outcomes. It reduces the pressure to force dramatic shifts that the psychological system is not ready to sustain. It also creates space to recognize progress where it actually occurs, rather than only where it is easiest to measure.

The next chapter turns to a broader cultural dynamic that often works against these slower, more realistic forms of change. It examines how debunking culture and moralized correction can unintentionally fuel the very beliefs they aim to suppress.

CHAPTER 14
Why Debunking Culture Backfires

Why Debunk Culture Backfires

Debunking culture is built on a straightforward assumption. If false claims are publicly corrected with clear evidence, people will update their beliefs and move closer to accurate understanding. This assumption fits a rationalist model of cognition. It treats belief as primarily a function of information quality. In practice, this model consistently fails in high-identity, high-threat contexts.

When correction becomes moralized, it stops functioning as information exchange and becomes a form of status enforcement. Public debunking often carries an implicit message about intelligence, morality, and group membership. The person being corrected is not just told that a claim is false. They are shown that they are wrong in a way that threatens their social standing. This transforms correction into a face-threatening act, which reliably activates defensive processes.

Identity warfare is one of the most damaging consequences of moralized correction. Once belief becomes associated with group identity, correcting the belief is experienced as attacking the group. Evidence is no longer evaluated on its merits. It is evaluated based on whether it comes from an in-group or an out-group. This dynamic turns factual disagreement into tribal conflict. In that environment, rejecting evidence can feel like loyalty, and accepting evidence can feel like betrayal.

Status threat amplifies this effect. When people feel that their social position, competence, or dignity is at risk, they become more invested in narratives that protect face. Public correction, especially when it is framed as obvious or humiliating, increases the psychological cost of changing one's mind. The person is asked not only to revise a belief, but to accept a loss of status. Many people will tolerate factual error longer than they will tolerate perceived humiliation.

Public shaming dynamics further entrench belief. When individuals are mocked, exposed, or portrayed as examples of ignorance, the social environment becomes hostile to doubt. Admitting uncertainty becomes dangerous. Retrenchment becomes safer. In these contexts, people may double down publicly even if they have private doubts, because public reversal would carry too much social cost. This creates a gap between private flexibility and public rigidity.

Debunking culture also incentivizes evangelizing. When people feel attacked, they often respond by recruiting others to validate their position. Sharing the belief becomes a way of restoring dignity and demonstrating commitment. What began as a defensive response becomes a form of identity performance. The belief spreads not because it has become more persuasive, but because it has become more emotionally and socially useful.

Another unintended consequence is the simplification of complex issues into binary frames. Debunking culture often rewards certainty and speed. Nuance is harder to communicate in viral formats. This encourages people to adopt more extreme and totalizing positions, because those positions are easier to defend and easier to signal. Over time, this escalates polarization and reduces the space for ambivalence or partial agreement.

These dynamics help explain why some correction efforts appear to make beliefs more visible and more intense. The correction itself becomes part of the narrative. It is incorporated as evidence of persecution, suppression, or elite control. In that way, debunking can be absorbed into the belief system it is trying to dismantle.

None of this means that false claims should be left unchallenged in public discourse. It does mean that the manner, context, and social meaning of correction matter as much as the content. Correction that humiliates, polarizes, or threatens identity is likely to strengthen the belief's psychological and social function, even if it is factually accurate.

Understanding why debunking culture backfires helps clarify earlier chapters. It shows why restraint, indirect engagement, and relational preservation are not signs of weakness. They are often strategically and ethically wiser approaches. They reduce the identity and status costs of flexibility, making it psychologically safer for people to loosen their grip on rigid narratives.

The next chapter turns to a broader question. If conspiracy thinking is partly a response to uncertainty, threat, and institutional breakdown, then reducing the demand for these narratives requires more than individual-level intervention. It requires building psychological and cultural resilience.

CHAPTER 15
Building Psychological Resilience

Building Psychological Resilience

If conspiracy thinking is partly a response to chronic uncertainty, perceived threat, and institutional breakdown, then reducing its prevalence requires more than correcting individual beliefs. It requires increasing the psychological and cultural capacity to live with ambiguity, complexity, and incomplete knowledge without needing totalizing narratives to stabilize experience.

Uncertainty tolerance is foundational. Many people experience uncertainty as psychologically intolerable. They feel pressure to resolve ambiguity quickly, even if the resolution is inaccurate. Strengthening uncertainty tolerance means helping individuals and communities develop the ability to hold unanswered questions without panic or collapse. This includes normalizing not knowing, reducing the stigma associated with ambivalence, and modeling how responsible adults manage incomplete information. When uncertainty becomes survivable, the emotional demand for rigid explanatory systems decreases.

Narrative humility is closely related. Narrative humility is the capacity to hold one's own story about the world with provisional confidence rather than absolute certainty. It does not mean abandoning convictions. It means recognizing that any single narrative is partial, shaped by perspective, and subject to revision. Cultures that reward narrative humility create space for disagreement without identity threat. In those environments, changing one's mind does not automatically imply weakness or betrayal. It becomes a sign of intellectual and emotional maturity.

Meaning systems that do not require enemies are another protective factor. Many conspiracy narratives derive power from defining a clear villain. The story becomes emotionally satisfying because it locates suffering in the actions of a malevolent other. Societies and subcultures that offer meaning through shared purpose, service, creativity, or collective problem-solving reduce the need for adversarial identity. When meaning is available without scapegoating, fewer people need narratives organized around hidden enemies to make sense of distress.

Cultural and institutional conditions also matter. High levels of corruption, inconsistency, secrecy, and perceived elite unaccountability create fertile ground for conspiratorial explanations. When institutions communicate poorly, contradict themselves, or appear indifferent to ordinary people's experiences, trust erodes. In those contexts, conspiracy narratives can feel more emotionally truthful than official accounts, even when they are factually unsupported. Improving transparency, accountability, and responsiveness is not just good governance. It is psychological prevention.

Media ecosystems play a role as well. Algorithmic systems that reward outrage, certainty, and moral polarization amplify the most emotionally charged content. This creates an environment where rigid narratives are more visible and more socially reinforced. Supporting media literacy, diversifying information sources, and reducing reliance on platforms that reward extremity can modestly reduce exposure to belief-reinforcing loops.

Psychological resilience is not a personality trait. It is a set of capacities shaped by social norms, institutions, and lived experience. When people feel secure, respected, and able to influence their environment in small but meaningful ways, they are less likely to require grand explanatory systems to maintain psychological equilibrium. When people feel chronically powerless, humiliated, or excluded, the psychological demand for totalizing narratives increases.

This chapter does not offer a simple program for eliminating conspiracy thinking. It reframes the problem. Rather than asking how to stamp out false beliefs, it asks how to build conditions in which rigid explanatory systems are less necessary. It treats conspiracy narratives as signals of deeper stress rather than isolated cognitive errors.

Building resilience is slower and less dramatic than public debunking. It does not produce viral moments. It does not generate the satisfaction of visible wins. It works at the level of capacity rather than correction. Over time, however, it changes the emotional landscape in which beliefs take root.

The final chapter draws these threads together. It states clearly what this book ultimately argues about conspiracy thinking, persuasion, and psychological maturity in an era of breakdowns in shared standards of truth and trust.

CHAPTER 16
What This Book Ultimately Argues

WHAT THIS BOOK ULTIMATELY ARGUES

What This Book Ultimately Argues

This book argues that conspiracy thinking is best understood not primarily as a defect in intelligence, education, or rationality, but as a functional psychological adaptation to environments marked by chronic uncertainty, threat, and breakdowns of trust. Many people who hold these beliefs are not confused, delusional, or cognitively impaired. They are responding to conditions that strain ordinary meaning-making systems. The beliefs persist because they do work. They regulate distress, restore a sense of agency, organize threat, and protect identity in contexts where other sources of stability feel unreliable or unavailable.

This functional perspective does not excuse harm. It explains persistence. It clarifies why facts alone rarely change minds. When a belief is serving core emotional and identity functions, disconfirmation threatens more than a proposition. It threatens psychological equilibrium. In those conditions, resistance is not stubbornness. It is self-protection.

The book also argues that the dominant cultural response to conspiracy thinking is ethically and psychologically flawed. Moralized certainty, public shaming, and status-based correction may feel justified, but they often strengthen the very dynamics they aim to dismantle. They increase identity threat, escalate tribal conflict, and raise the social cost of doubt. In doing so, they make rigid belief more psychologically necessary, not less.

Persuasion, in this context, has ethical limits. When engagement becomes an attempt to force belief change at the expense of psychological stability, dignity, or relationship, it can become a form of coercion rather than care. This is especially true in clinical and relational settings, where the goal is not to win battles over what's true, but to support functioning, safety, and long-term flexibility. The book argues that there are times when restraint is not avoidance, but responsibility.

At the same time, the book draws clear boundaries. When conspiracy beliefs become vehicles for medical danger, coercion, abuse, violence, or severe functional impairment, neutrality is not ethical. Protective intervention is required. Psychological understanding does not override the obligation to prevent harm. The

What This Book Ultimately Argues

functional account is not a moral blank check. It is a framework for distinguishing between situations where indirect, relational, and capacity-building approaches are appropriate and situations where direct action is necessary.

A central claim of this book is that belief change is often the wrong primary metric for success. Reduced rigidity, decreased preoccupation, increased tolerance for ambivalence, and restored functioning are frequently more meaningful indicators of psychological movement than public renunciation of a narrative. Softening, not conversion, is often the realistic path toward greater flexibility and reduced harm.

The book also argues that conspiracy thinking is not just an individual psychological issue. It is a cultural signal. High levels of uptake point to environments in which uncertainty is overwhelming, institutions are distrusted, and people feel stripped of agency and dignity. Reducing the demand for conspiracy narratives requires addressing these conditions, not just correcting the stories that grow out of them.

Underlying all of this is a broader claim about psychological maturity in an era of breakdowns in shared standards of truth and trust. Maturity is not defined by perfect certainty or flawless information processing. It is defined by the capacity to live with incomplete knowledge, tolerate ambiguity, revise narratives without humiliation, and hold disagreement without turning it into identity warfare. It involves recognizing the limits of one's own certainty and resisting the pull toward totalizing explanations that promise emotional relief at the cost of flexibility.

This book ultimately argues that restraint can be more responsible than confrontation, not because truth does not matter, but because how truth is held, communicated, and enforced shapes whether it becomes a tool for understanding or a weapon for domination. Psychological care, ethical engagement, and social responsibility require more than being right. They require understanding what beliefs are doing for the people who hold them and choosing responses that reduce harm rather than escalate it.

The cost of moralized certainty is high. It fractures relationships, entrenches identity conflict, and turns deep disagreements about what's true into moral combat. In environments already saturated with threat and instability, this dynamic accelerates polarization and increases the psychological demand for rigid narratives.

What this book offers is not a technique for eliminating conspiracy thinking. It offers a framework for responding to it with greater precision, humility, and ethical clarity. It invites readers to distinguish between explanation and endorsement, between restraint and complicity, between care and control.

In an era where certainty is rewarded and complexity is punished, psychological maturity may look quieter and less satisfying. It may involve holding unresolved questions, tolerating discomfort, and resisting the urge to convert every disagreement into a test of virtue. This book argues that such maturity is not weakness. It is one of the few reliable ways to reduce harm, preserve human connection, and remain psychologically grounded in a world where clear answers are often unavailable.

When The System Is The Target

THE END

www.ingramcontent.com/pod-product-compliance
Lightning Source LLC
Chambersburg PA
CBHW070644030426
42337CB00020B/4150